Breaking Down the Greatest Show on Turf

Unauthorized X's and O's: Volume I

Alex Kirby

CONTENTS

i

1
QUICK PASSES

The ability of Kurt Warner to get rid of the football not only accurately but on time is of paramount importance to the success of this offense.

In an age before the bubble screen come into vogue for offenses at all levels of football, Mike Martz and this Rams offense found lots of creative ways to attack defenses from all kinds of formations.

As you'll see in this first chapter, the offense uses different concepts, sometimes putting them on opposite sides of the formation to account for different contingencies.

Shallow Cross/Angle Route

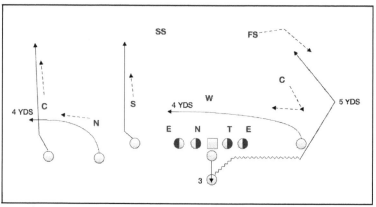

This is one of the many ways Mike Martz would regularly try to get his guys not only open past a certain point, but if possible, a free release off the line of scrimmage that will let them build up speed and momentum as he's gaining depth on the play.

Offensive coaches have been stacking and bunching receivers together for decades to negate the effect of press man coverage, and superior talent at the defensive back position.

When you add premier talent at the skill positions to a scheme designed to maximize talent, good things are bound to happen.

The defense is trying to play a 2-deep look to this trips formation, at least before the ball is snapped, since they want to remain as vague as possible about what they're trying to accomplish.

By starting out in a trips set and then moving to an empty look, the Rams are putting all kinds of stress on the defense, and make it nearly impossible for their opponent to disguise coverages and their overall intentions.

When the offense motions the tailback out of the backfield, and flexes him out as the widest man to that side, he brings the free safety with him, instantly confirming that the defense is lining up in man coverage.

At this point, before the snap, the quarterback should be aware of the matchups on individual defenders, especially those this team has game planned for, as well as the leverage any one man has on his defender once the defense has declared their intentions.

The late-developing angle route from Faulk was a reliable play call for St. Louis many, many times back in their heyday.

Shallow/Angle Combination

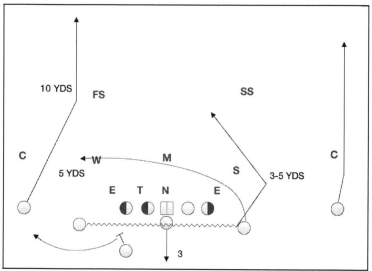

This play is the next step in the progression of attacking the middle of the field, and different defenders with regards to the structure of the formation.

With the Z receiver split out wide to the right, the corner is occupied by the vertical route, and depending on the leverage of the strong safety, the Sam linebacker may be isolated over the top of the Z-receiver combination all alone.

To the left side of the play, the vertical route by the X receiver does the same job as the Z receiver, clearing out members of the secondary to the left. What you often end up having on this play is a scheme designed to open up the middle of the field, and to unleash a pair of wide receivers on the guys underneath, linebackers who are ill-equipped to play out in space and cover bigger and faster receivers with great hands.

The angle route comes underneath the drag route on the release off the line of scrimmage, and the drag route, while not explicitly intended as a sacrificial lamb to occupy the underneath coverage, it often works out that way.

Even if the Sam linebacker doesn't necessarily chase one route or the other, standing in place with his eyes on the quarterback, it's still easy for the receiver on the angle route to avoid him and find the open window in the zone.

The read is simplified by the split of the outside receivers to either side, and by watching the defense's reaction to the man in motion, Warner can get a pretty good idea of what the picture is going to look like after the snap.

A second passing window will emerge in the deep middle of the field as it relates to the drop (or lack thereof) of the middle linebacker.

It's also important to coach up the drag route across the middle as well, since even though it's drawn up as a regular drag across the field right where the Will linebacker is sitting, the reality is that a smart receiver will have to read the drop of the Will as he's coming across the middle, and be ready for the football sometime after he passes the Mike. Finding that hole in the underneath coverage is essential to getting open for a pass (and preventing your head from being knocked off).

Trips Smash/ X Slant

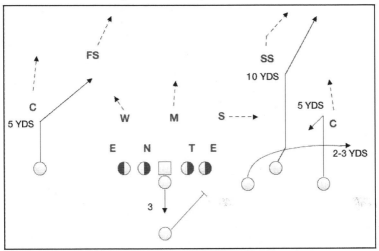

The emphasis on quick passes is all about getting the ball out, well, quickly. As a result, there is often not enough time to scan the entire field unless the routes are spread out in a specific way, and Warner is forced to pick a side before the ball is snapped.

In this case of the diagram, the defense is playing their linebackers especially tight to the tackle box, not spacing themselves out appropriately and leaving lots of room to the trips side outside to the right.

With the Sam linebacker playing inside of the #3 receiver, the flat route instantly has an advantage already, with leverage on the nearest inside defender. With the way the defense is playing against this concept, the offense actually has a 3 on 2 advantage to the outside, and the corner is dropping, along with the strong safety to double the corner route. The offense has all kinds of opportunities to the right side, but in this particular situation Warner is eyeing the slant side of the formation.

QB coaches will tell their group that when trying to throw the slant, there are two different slant "windows" as the receiver goes through the route, and it's all dependent on the leverage of the underneath defender, in this case, the Will linebacker.

The first window appears just as the X receiver is making his first break to the inside, particularly against tight man coverage by the corner playing over the top of him, and it closes once the underneath defender gets in position to undercut the route.

Once the slant route comes over the top of the Will linebacker, that's when the second window appears. Since the Mike linebacker opens up to the strong side to wall off any potential in-breaking routes coming from the trips side, it's a matter of getting open underneath against the Will linebacker.

HB Wheel Z Sit

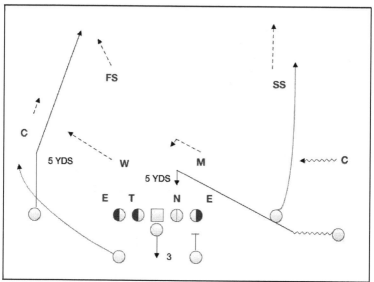

On this example of the play, the defense screwed up and left only ten men on the field.

This is an example of a play that could turn into either a quick pass or a more vertical, downfield throw.

The offense brings the Z receiver in short motion to almost a stacked position underneath the tight end who is flexed out.

Warner gets rid of the ball on his 3rd step to the back wheeling out to the flat once he sees the flat open up, if even for a second. It's cover 2, so the corner comes back down to the wheel route.

He ends up short-arming the throw (or just putting the ball where only the back had a chance to get it).

He's reading left-to-right, peeking first at the route by the X, then to the wheel route, and if both of those are covered, the Z should sit down in the middle of the field and offer a safe, high-percentage throw.

The concept puts a great horizontal stretch on the left side of the defense, and the late arrival of the Z receiver to that side of the field presents the defense with a big challenge in covering everyone and clamping down on the pass just long enough for the pass rush to get there.

Empty Texas/ Fade-Out

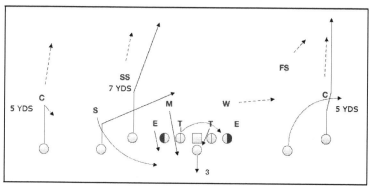

There are a couple of things to account for on this play, and they are happening on both sides of the play, and they are happening on both sides of the ball.

First of all before we start to pay attention to what the offense is doing let's talk about the alignment of the defenders to both sides, and what their intentions are. It's best to think of this empty set as two separate formations, and draw on invisible line down the middle of the center.

Notice to the Z receiver side that the Will linebacker is neatly tucked into the tackle box, leaving the #2 receiver uncovered at first glance. Conversely, though we can see from the diagram that the pressure is coming from the left side, the alignment of the Sam is wide enough to hopefully disarm any thought is Warner's mind that there is pressure coming from that side.

Meanwhile, with the Will aligned so tight to the box, the defense is hoping to convince Warner to throw to the #2 "hot" off the blitz where the Will who originally was thought to be the blitzer flies out and makes the tackle after a gain of 1-2 yards.

Now we get to the actual offensive play call.

This is a modified version of the Texas concept that this offense makes a habit of including in their game plan out of different formations and backfield sets.

The middle receiver running the angle route that breaks into the middle of the field underneath the vertical release of the tight end on the skinny post. It's worth mentioning that the angle route is normally timed up to delay his break over the middle as if he was running the route starting from the backfield.

In this example, Warner recognizes the trap the defense is trying to spring on him, and gets the ball off to the angle route, and St. Louis picks up a huge gain after the catch.

Mirrored Smash Concepts

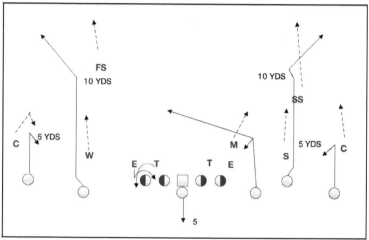

A quick glance at this diagram should tell you that with a smash concept to either side, the offense is attempting to cut the field in half and simplify the reads for Warner, as well as challenge the defense deep.

The St. Louis offense routinely defied convention, and a great example is the way they were able to attack down the field out of the empty set with such great protection and talented skill players.

Of course, with the two mirrored concepts wide to either side, the question becomes, how do you keep the middle of the defense honest? The last thing you want is the defenders in the middle of the field left to their own devices, free to read the quarterback's eyes and get a jump on wherever he decides to throw it.

That's where the route by the #3 receiver to the right side comes into play.

In the diagram, you can see that the Mike linebacker is aligned to his inside before the snap, trying his best to take away the easy throw over the middle, expecting a quick release from Warner.

Instead, the receiver sits down at five yards running the hitch route, and once the Mike is on top of him threatening to take away the passing lane, the receiver sprints to the wide open middle of the field, where Warner can hit him in stride for a big gain.

Routes like this one are a great example of how important practice reps and chemistry are to developing an elite passing attack. Warner and this receiving corps have to be on the same page at all times in order to have this ability as the play is going on.

Like a lot of concepts in this offense, there isn't really a wrong answer here, it all depends on where your progression starts as a passer, and what the defense decides to take away.

Against a lot of defenses, Warner would probably be alright trying to throw the smash concept, but in the defense drawn up in this particular diagram, the outside linebackers are helping to take away the routes and outnumber the offense to the perimeter, which is where the outlet pass is so valuable.

.

2
MOVEMENT PASSES

You probably don't remember Kurt Warner as a "running QB," and you'd be right. Warner made his living picking apart defenses from inside the pocket.

An examination of this offense would be incomplete, however, without looking at the play design that moved the pocket around and forced Warner to use his legs a little bit.

Plays like these are less about forcing the defense to account for Warner's limited ability in the running game, and more about moving the pocket around.

You want to present a moving target to the defense, especially the pass rushers up front, so that they can't just get down in a sprinters stance and tee off on your quarterback. When combined with a healthy dose of the quick passing game, which we covered in the previous chapter, it adds up to a game plan that keeps your quarterback healthy and upright.

Good playcallers understand this, and it's why even in a league dominated by pocket passers today, you'll see quarterbacks rolling out or booting off a run fake to create hesitation in the defense.

This approach isn't unique to Martz and his philosophy, but he does have his own ways of going about it. His playbook is specifically set up to take advantage of the talent he has at his disposal, which is what we'll cover in this chapter.

It's worth noting as well, what we're talking about when we use the term "Movement Passes." For our purposes, the term can mean any pass play where the quarterback is assigned to leave the pocket. This could be a sprint out to one side or another, or he could be faking a handoff in one direction and booting out to the other.

The important characteristic is that the quarterback is on the move, either leaving the pocket entirely, or sometimes, moving out to the edge and bringing a few blockers with him.

The offense works to continue to give the defense a moving target, so let's take a look at a couple of examples.

Sprint Out Hitch and Go

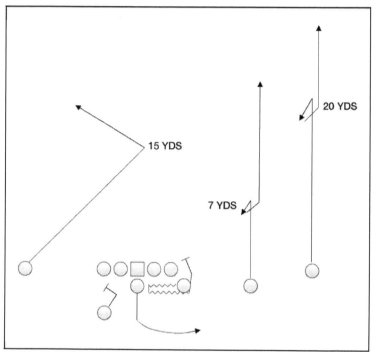

This play is best understood as a constraint against aggressive defenses, especially those corners and safeties who pride themselves on preparing for an opponent down to every last detail and recognizing a play as it develops. In fact, these sort of plays actually work *better* against smart players, since those are exactly the kinds of players who would use what they know to anticipate what happens next.

It's the same sort of counter-intuitive thinking that says the best defense to run misdirection plays against is a speedy one, since the faster a defense plays, the faster they can get out of position.

Note the spacing of the routes, not only horizontally, but also vertically, so that the double moves are designed to make their move against the defenders at different intervals. The routes are timed up to be in sync with Warner's path rolling out to the edge.

The hope is that the defenders over each of these routes will try to sit on them, and come over the top of the receiver, thus losing all momentum and allowing the receiver to go deep undefended.

The backside route that usually comes over the deep middle on so many of these sprint out and boot plays, should get to the middle of the field at a fifteen yard depth, then pivot and head back the other way on a corner route.

This is a way to control the free safety, especially if he has a tendency to do what the defenders to the frontside of the play are being lured into doing.

Thus, the Rams have the ability to call this play with either outcome in mind, to either take advantage of defenders to the playside who like to jump the routes in front of them, or attack the deep middle of the secondary who gets lazy

Sprint Right Option

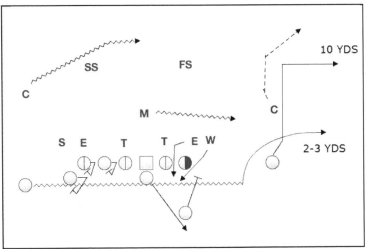

This is a play built into just about every pro passing playbook out there, and like a lot of successful passing concepts in the league (and several in this book) they have their roots in the Bill Walsh passing attack.

Called "sprint right option" in the original West Coast Offense, this concept was responsible for Dwight Clark making "the Catch" against the Cowboys in the 1981 NFC Championship.

Starting with the tailback in the offset position to the weak side of the formation. His only job is to secure the edge as Warner sprints out to the right, especially in this case as the defense brings the Will linebacker off the edge into the C gap.

A reliable blitz key from the defense is who they use to adjust to motion. In this case, St. Louis brings the Z receiver across the formation to get into the position to run the flat route underneath the vertical release of the outside receiver running the deep out route. When the defense brings the Mike linebacker is motion to mirror the movement of the Z receiver, and leaves the Will linebacker in place in his position on the edge, Faulk and warner should be expecting some kind of Will pressure coming from that side of the formation.

The emphasis on the play is finding a way to get the football to the Z receiver on the flat route. By getting your receiver matched up on a Mike linebacker, there's automatically a speed mis-match as he moves to the outside.

Meanwhile, the outside receiver is running the deep out route, and depending on the leverage of the corner playing across from him, could also break open at 10 yards.

The tight ends and the offensive line to the backside of the play work as a team t seal off the inside gaps and prevent any penetration by defenders chasing Warner down from that side.

The other question when game planning and deciding whether or not to throw the deep out route is how the near safety will defend the route to his side.

Since there is no route coming from the backside of the formation to hold the defenders in the middle of the field, the safeties can play extra aggressive to the side of the sprint out.

In reality the safety shouldn't matter, since the goal is to get the football out quickly to the flat, and if he's covered, to the out route shortly after that.

3
PLAY-PASSES

So let's build on the idea of the movement pass and how it fits into the game plan, by introducing the play-pass.

Football fans everywhere are familiar with the term playaction, where the quarterback pretends to hand off the ball on a running play, only to end up throwing it instead.

Fewer fans, however, are as familiar with the play-pass.

The term playaction is used whenever there's any kind of ball fake, no matter what the rest of the play entails. A play-pass on the other hand, describes a specific kind of playaction fake where the quarterback doesn't boot out, but stays in the pocket instead, and does very little moving around before getting rid of the football.

To build off of our discussion about movement passes in the last chapter, this is the other side of the coin.

These kinds of plays are the natural complements to a power or isolation play, where generally a quarterback will fake the run straight up the middle.

So let's get into a few examples of how this Rams offense uses this part of the gameplan.

Post-Wheel-Delay

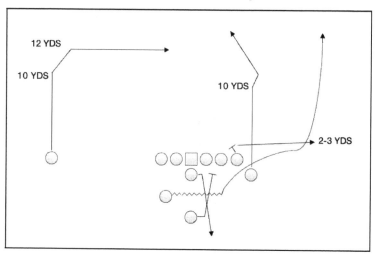

In this scenario, St. Louis packages their power run game with a great vertical passing concept designed to attack the strong side of the formation.

A common theme in this offense is to run passing concepts that create natural rubs on defenders, as well as creating "bunch-like" concepts out of non-bunch formations. This is particularly the case in this phase of the offense, since the backfield action of carrying out a play fake marries up so well with running flat routes. Once you add another route to the play that creates a natural rub in conjunction with the flat route, you've got a great way to create hesitation on defense, as well as possibly spring one of your receivers free against press man coverage.

On this play, the offense comes out on to the field with 22 personnel and creates a wing alignment to the strong side of the formation. After bringing the fullback in motion from left to right, the offense creates a bunch look out of an original formation.

The progression reads from high to low on this play, with the dig route from the single receiver side used as an "alert" as well as a way to influence the middle of the field coverage and open a passing lane for the post route breaking into the deep middle.

The wheel route coming out of the backfield should break vertical once he gets to the bottom of the numbers, then make a rounded turn while keeping a decent distance from the sideline. The formation and route concept are designed to create a compressed look with the tight end/wing alignment, bringing the corner in tight to the edge and opening up lots of room to the outside and behind him as he hopefully drops with the post route and brackets the vertical route in conjunction with a defender playing inside leverage.

Meanwhile, the attached tight end runs a delay route into the flat that is timed up to hit once the other two routes have gone vertical and cleared out the coverage.

Obviously the play fake helps control the coverage, which provides an opportunity to get the football early to the post route before he makes his break at ten yards.

Twins "Star" Concept

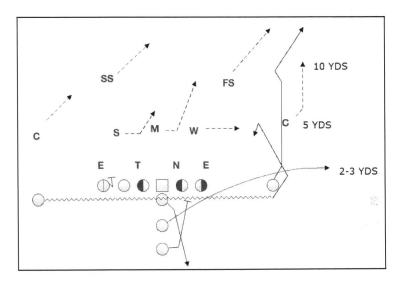

This is a great way to move from an I-formation into a position where the offense has the ability to run a bunch route.

There are many different versions of this concept, and where most coaches make the biggest changes has to do with the route by the Z receiver, or in other words, the in-breaking route in the concept.

There are a lot of coaches who view this guy as a primarily a sacrificial lamb, a route designed to create a rub on the defender covering the out-

31

breaking route, and create an open receiver in the flat. In this case, the in-breaking receiver still runs a path where he can interfere with a defender flying out to the flat, but at the same time he creates enough separation between himself and the other receiver to present himself as a viable receiving threat.

The vertical route by the receiver at the "point" of the bunch route follows the typical pattern of running a corner route, by adding a bit of hesitation at the top of the route at the point where he breaks it back out to the sideline.

Defensive coordinators have several different ways to defend these concepts, which leads us to another reason why it's to the advantage of the offense to line up in the I-Formation originally, the moving the stacked twins alignment. For one thing, a popular adjustment is to line up a defender, either a linebacker or a safety, over the point of the bunch to create a lot of resistance at the line of scrimmage, and put a lot of pressure on the other two receivers to get to their assigned landmarks on time, since both of them must come underneath the release of the point man.

As you can see from the diagrams the defense doesn't have the time to adjust to the motion and play the stacked alignment by putting someone over the top of the "point" man.

Both the corner and the near safety will drop deep, bracketing the corner route and taking away both sides of it so that there is no comfortable place for the QB to put the football.

In this case, the sit-down route provides enough of a "screen" for the fullback running out into the flat to create space for an easy completion.

Play Action Post-Dig Concept

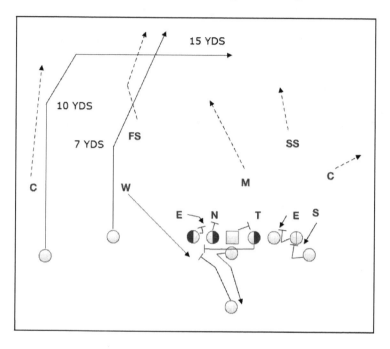

In what's quickly becoming a theme in this section of the book, the offense brings in a couple of big guys to create a good look for a play fake, then keeps a lot of guys in the block and give Warner all kinds of time to find guys down the field as his receivers stretch the defense and attack deep.

At the snap, Warner drops back and opens to his left to carry out the play fake to Faulk. At the same time, the right guard pulls to the left to add a more convincing look to the backfield, and both he and Faulk set up to the left to create a longer to protect Warner.

Meanwhile, to the right side of the formation, a similar action is taking shape. These two tight ends to the "wing" side of the formation are trying to accomplish two things. They want to shore up any open space (along with the right tackle) that could've been created when the right guard pulled to the left to block out on any edge pressure coming from the left side. They also are trying to create another lengthy edge to the right side to protect Warner as he's waiting for his receivers to get open.

In this case, the defense brings the Will linebacker off the edge, and because of the backfield action that brings the tailback and the right guard to the left edge, he's easily picked up.

Now to the pass concept.

This concept is specifically designed to hi-lo the near safety, or the first guy they find defending the deep middle of the field.

The slot receiver running the post route on a very skinny angle breaks at about 7 yards, and ultimately his job in the play is to get over the top of the near safety, which puts the safety in a bind once the dig route comes across the middle at a 15 yard depth.

The obvious issue for the defender is what to do when you've got two routes coming into your area. The simplest answer is to stay deeper than the deepest receiver to your side. In that case, against a 2-deep shell, the receiver running the dig route should throttle down in the open space in the middle of the field.

Another thing that can be helpful for the defense is the speed and awareness of the linebackers underneath, and in this scenario the Mike linebacker recognizes the play, dropping into the passing lane as he reads Warner's eyes.

Fake Toss X Slant

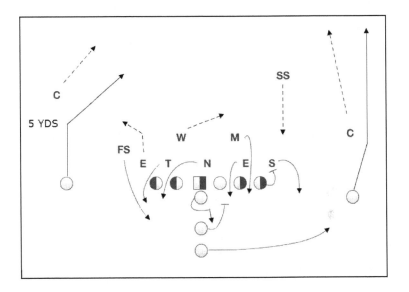

This is a great changeup to the type of run-pass packaged play that is often paired up with run schemes that involve pulling guards, especially on the power play, and it continually runs the risk of creating a mishap in the backfield if the guard and quarterback's footwork aren't perfect every time.

By faking the toss play, the offense has the advantage of having a similar backfield action where the quarterback opens up in a counter-clockwise to fake the run play, and then coming around again in pass position to hit the backside slant route, which at the same time you're not pulling anyone on the offensive line, which means that you're not at risk of any "friendly fire" or unwanted collisions in the backfield between offensive linemen and the quarterback since you're not pulling any offensive linemen.

As for the rest of the reads in the pass game, this is a classic left-to-right progression, where the tailback comes back into play as the final outlet in the progression.

This is all a process that should happen in the span of less than two seconds, since the offensive line is coming off the line of scrimmage with such force and aggressiveness that other than securing their inside gap, their primary assignment is to present a run-first look to the defense, not creating a secure pocket for Warner to sit and back and scan the defense for a long time.

The whole point of the play is to create enough hesitation at the linebacker position to open up the passing lane for the slant route so that the passer can get the ball past them.

Play Action Z Deep Out

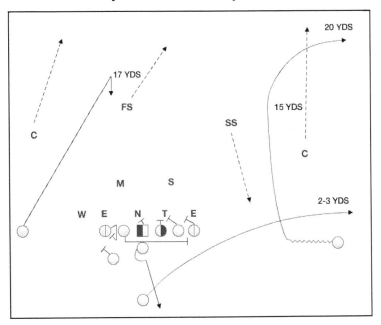

Not as complex when it comes to the progression on this play compared with others in this section.

Pairing the power scheme with a vertical passing concept, St. Louis uses this play to get the football to a designated receiver deep down the sideline, but also has the ability to get the ball to the X receiver whose job is to search out an open spot deep in the middle of the field.

Just like many other instances in this offense, the reason to bring the receiver in short motion is to create lots of space for him to the outside. He's in a spot pre-snap where it looks like he's getting ready to get downfield and get a body on the strong safety just like in the run game.

Pulling the guard is a large part of the deception, since you've got a combination of the tight end blocking down and the guard pulling around to the edge of the line of scrimmage to kick out any edge rushers and create a secure pocket for Warner to set up and wait for his receivers to come open.

The fullback's alignment in the backfield is also set up in a great position to deal with any penetration from the defense on the left side of the offensive line because of the open space that's created when the guard pulls to the edge.

Another interesting wrinkle is that the back heading out to the flat is coming from the tailback position. Part of this is because of the special talent they've at that position in Marshall Faulk. By having Faulk shoot to the perimeter underneath, not only does St. Louis get one of their best players in space out of the backfield action of the play fake, but they also hope to catch someone in the secondary peeking into the backfield.

This play call can be especially effective if Faulk has already made a couple of big plays earlier in the game, especially on screen plays or by making catches out of the backfield, that have led to some big gains. Whenever you can create hesitation in the defense, either with play action, or just by giving the defense a look that frightens them a bit, you're doing your job as a play caller.

4
SHIFTS & MOTIONS

Football is a game not just of strength and toughness, but also of deception.

In the game's earliest days, when the forward pass was still looked upon as a gimmick play, Notre Dame Head Coach Knute Rockne utilized an offensive set that became known as the Notre Dame Box.

In this offense, the team would line up in on formation, then send multiple players in motion just before the ball was snapped, so that in essence they would end up in an entirely different set before the defense knew what had happened (This tactic was later made illegal).

These days, you're allowed to move multiple players around before the snap, but they must come to a stop and stand still for a full second before either sending someone else in motion or snapping the ball.

Within the modern framework available to them, teams still have the ability to create confusion and move players around before the snap, but few coaches in the modern era have embraced this phase of the game the way Martz did in the late 90s and early 2000s.

Having dangerous players at the skill positions is one thing, but add to that the ability to move them around and create confusion so that the opposing defense is never sure what's up, and you have a recipe offensive dominance.

Z Motion to Curl-Wheel-Flare

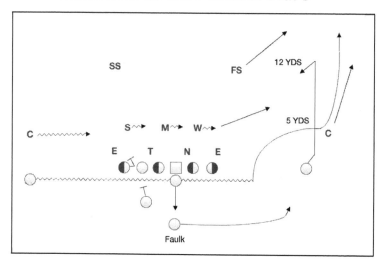

This is a great example of using simple motion against a base 4-3 defense that was even more common during this time in pro football.

This is when it's important to keep the formation, personnel, and the situation in mind when analyzing the play. The movement of the Z receiver in motion across the formation, the movement (or lack thereof) of the Will linebacker is kept to a minimum by his responsibility to stay gap sound against the two-back set that St. Louis has lined up in because they've got a fullback on the field and give the defense a run look.

From an alignment standpoint, it's also good to have Faulk lined up at the tailback position, in other words, he's centrally-located, and like so many other plays in this offense, it allows St. Louis to create "bunch-type" routes out of typical two-back formations.

There are plenty of teams who simply run the curl route combined with a flat route (originating from within the backfield or from a slot receiver), but by converting the flat route to a wheel route, then inserting the flare route to a wheel route, then inserting the flare route late to replace that space, you're able to overload the defense to that side.

A common adjustment to an offense moving to the Twins formation is to bring pressure from the tight end side, since most teams are either trying to set up the run to the tight end side, or are targeting the Twins side in the pass game.

There's also the question of how a defense will adjust to the Z receivers coming in motion across the formation and moves to Twins, because as we've talked about before, the Will linebacker has a job to do first and foremost in the run game.

Certainly those are defensive coordinators who will cheat that outside linebacker a few extra steps toward the Twins side, but they still have to be accountable in the run game, and depending on the kind of talent you have at that position, it's not necessarily the case that you'll be able to play both the run and the pass well.

Something has to give, and by widening out the Will linebacker it creates an opportunity in the run game to that side. Of course the other option is to make some kind of adjustment with the secondary, usually by rotating the safety down.

This is exactly why a guy like Martz likes to put his receivers in motion out of this formation, because it puts the run support defenders in such a bind.

Tight End Shift and Four Verticals

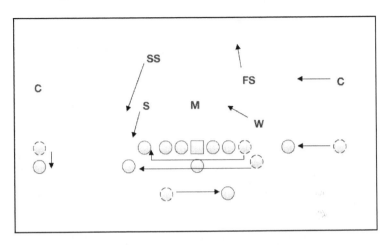

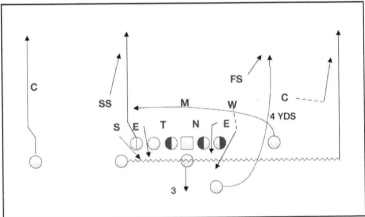

Not only does the offense switch up their alignments, but the strength of the offense is flipped as well, which is something to keep in mind as we go through this section.

This play is similar to others in the book, and the tight alignment of the receiver to the right side provides a natural rub for the back as he's shooting out of the backfield and flying down the seams matched up against the safety.

The most noticeable effect or the defense is that the safeties switch up their alignments, since the safety to the tight end/wing side plays a lot lower into the tackle box to account for the run. There's also the outside linebackers who switch up their alignments playing up on the line of scrimmage, which also has to do with the location of the tight end.

This is another way to run the four verticals concept out of a more unorthodox alignment.

Then, once the 2nd tight end comes in motion across the formation and lines up far to the right side to get matched up on the corner to that side, as well as stretching out the interior of the defense.

Because of the width of Faulk's release, he is leaving the door open for the tight end to run a seam route down the middle, and leaves plenty of room for Warner to throw the route open.

Meanwhile, the shallow crossing route underneath for the Mike linebacker, as well as the route that comes open once he clears the vertical release of the tight end to the other side.

In this particular situation, the defense comes with pressure off of both sides, but the play is designed and timed up to get the football out quickly.

This is another area where the shallow crossing route comes into play, since as soon as the receiver breaks underneath and sees the mean outside linebacker comes on the blitz, he should expect the football right away just as he's breaking inside at the 3-4 yard mark.

It's important to recognize the importance of having such a strong offensive line. Orlando Pace was responsible at left tackle for a lot of wins in St. Louis, just because of his legendary ability to neutralize the opposing pass rush. This gives Mike Martz the ability to release four, or on this occasion, five receivers out into the pass pattern. This makes it very tough to outnumber the offense in the passing game when they have the ability to release as many people as possible.

Shift to Ace Y Shallow Cross

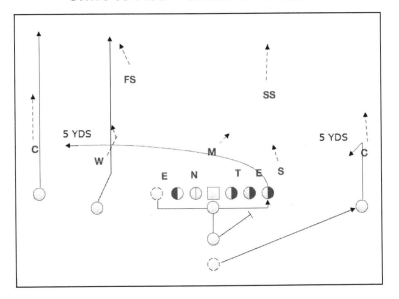

This play is a great example of not only the shifting around that was so key to the Rams' offensive success, but also a concept which is not discussed enough but is extremely important to success in any offense.

It's been described as a lot of things, but for our purposes we'll call it no-man's-land.

The goal of a good offensive coordinator should not only be to put as many of the defenders in a bind as possible, but also to get defenders in a position, at least in zone coverage, where they're not covering anyone.

This sometimes happens when you're forcing a group of lazy and undisciplined pass defenders, but can also come from an efficient play design.

This play gives a good example of how to get two defenders to cover a small patch of turf and basically take themselves out of the play.

At first, the offense is lined up in an unbalanced twins formation then suddenly, the tight end flips sides and the tailback Faulk goes wide and lines up in the flanker position to put the offense in a traditional one-back Ace set. Only the fullback remains in the backfield, still in his original position behind the quarterback.

The play is designed to clear out the coverage to the left side of the formations, by running both of the receivers deep and creating open space for the tight ends as he runs his crossing route underneath and over the middle.

As the tight end comes off the line of scrimmage, he is collisioned by the Sam linebacker, and also has the Mike linebacker to beat underneath. As he beats the initial resistance coming off the line, he finds all kinds of open space to the opposite side of the formation, especially if the Will is extra aggressive in his drops and attempt to control the release of the #2 receiver.

The two receiver side can also turn into the primary side in the progression depending on the situation and the kind of coverage being shown to that side. Against a press corner and a "Cover 2" look to that side, the Rams can find some good space at the intermediate level, either in the seams to #2, or in the hole in the coverage along the sideline between the corner and the safety.

As the very least, the QB's eyes should start at the two-receiver side to the pass defenders off the trail a bit, and times up the throw to the tight end that comes open late over the middle.

As far as the concept of no-man's-land that we talked about earlier, since the Mike is keeping one eye on the fullback as he shoots to the right, he and the Sam will be occupying a lot of the same space. As far as the Sam, he can't collision the tight end and provide support to the flat to help with the hitch route at the same time.

Regardless of how close the two of them are, by design they are taken out of the play and end up covering nothing but grass.

Shift To Splitbacks – Shallow Cross

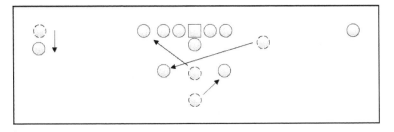

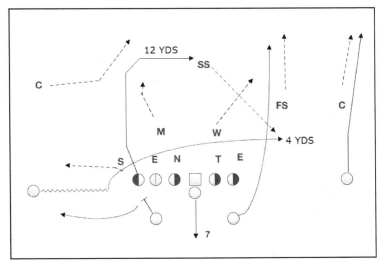

This one is a lot of fun to watch, but was kind of difficult to draw up.

The Rams start out in the I-Formation with a "flexed" look to the right side. Like most other shifts in this offense, the tight end moves into a spot that ends up changing the strength of the formation. In this case, the tight end starts out at the fullback position before setting up on the line of scrimmage right next to the left tackle.

At the same time, the back lined up in the slot to the right that gave the formation its original strength to the right, shifts back to an offset position in the backfield about 4-5 yards behind the left tackle.

Finally, Faulk, who was originally lined up in the tailback spot in the I-Formation backfield, now moves to the spot behind the right tackle to create a classic splitbacks look.

As has been mentioned in other places in this book, the short motion by the flanker in this offense, and in a lot of others, is a pretty reliable indicator for the defense that there is likely an in-breaking route, an out-breaking route, and a vertical route coming from that side of the formation.

As to who will be running what route, that's not necessarily a given, but it's almost a guarantee that certain players and routes will be switching up, and that one of them will be attacking the deep area of the field to that side. This explains why the corner begins to back up and gain depth as the flanker moves closer to the tight end.

To the opposite side of the formation, the two vertical routes that are customarily run down the field to clear out the underneath portion of the coverage.

In this case, the inside vertical route originates from Faulk lined up in the backfield. This gives the offense the ability to line up in a two-back set, which still being able to run a lot of the same passing concepts that are associated with one-back formations.

Running a vertical route out of the backfield also given the offense the ability to directly influence the Mike linebacker, since Faulk is the one he's staring at once the ball is snapped. As we can see from the diagram, both the free safety and the Mike linebacker are covering Faulk's vertical route, which is key.

Since the offense brings the flanker in tight to run a shallow crossing route, it makes sense that they'll also need a plan to make room for him once he makes the catch on the opposite side of the formation.

With both inside vertical routes being doubled by the linebackers and defensive backs to each side, the defense still finds a way to get a defender in place to make the tackle on the shallow crossing route after the catch.

As a defensive coach preparing for St. Louis, one question they've got to answer is how they're going to defend the shallow crossing route. It's important to understand where the catch is supposed to happen, and how the play is designed to create a lot of open space away from where the shallow cross comes from so that the receiver can make the catch and turn up the field.

The offense is trying to get the football to the receiver on the opposite hash make, so when the strong safety sees the flanker move in tight and the shallow crossing route starts to develop, he immediately vacates the middle of the field and runs to where he knows the route will end up.

Since both inside verticals are doubled already, the strong safety can roam around and attack where he thinks the football is going. As he takes a good angle to the end of the route, he has the ability to shut down any speed and momentum that the receiver has built up.

Because of the angle he takes to get in front of the route, he's either gonna be able to make the tackle, or at least turn the receiver back inside to the rest of the defense.

This is one of the more unorthodox adjustments to the offense's favorite play, but it's effective, and it forces Martz to dig deeper into his bag of tricks.

Now we come full circle to the reason why the movements of players before the snap is such a crucial part of this offense.

In a situation like this, where a defense was able to hone in so well on what to expect, so much so that disguising where players are going to be standing where the ball is snapped is of maximum importance.

At its core, this offense is built around a few solid principles, and in the age before no-huddle offenses became the norm, Mike Martz's offense represented a totally different school of thought on deceiving your opponent.

While these days most coaches prefer to move so fast that the defense doesn't have time to pick up on the lay coming next, Martz comes from the other side of the debate. While this offense certainly has the ability to speed things up if they need to, they'll still huddle and run at a more conventional tempo.

The deception is the offense comes from Martz's unique design and combinations of pre-snap movements, designed to obscure the offense's intentions, and make it harder for the defense to settle into whatever exotic calls they've got dialed up.

In this case, the defense sees through all the smoke and mirrors, which means St. Louis will have to find another way to get their receivers running free across the middle.

5
DROPBACK PASSING GAME

Now we come to the meat of the passing game, the dropback section of the playbook, and the one that is maximized not only by talented players at the skill positions, but also by dominant players on the offensive line.

A solid dropback passing game allows Warner time to sit back in the pocket, survey the defense, and wait for his guys to beat their man (which tended to happen a lot back in those days).

This chapter will introduce some of the most common dropback concepts in the Rams passing attack, before moving on to more specific areas within this part of the playbook.

Z Curl

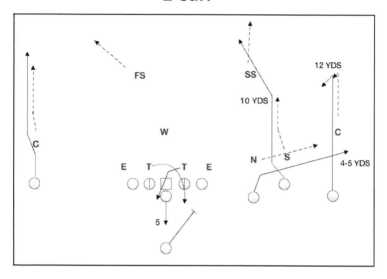

This is one of the most basic concepts in football, and one that has been around for a long time.

The curl concept to the trips side is designed so that the offense can attack both man and zone coverages.

Because of the width of the backside receiver to the single receiver side of the formation, in theory you could add any route as an adjustment to the blitz (hot receiver) or even getting the tailback involved on a 2-man combination. In this case, the fade route is there to occupy the backside safety, and also to provide alert throw for Warner if they find the defense is a little too fixated on the 3 receiver side.

Meanwhile, back to the frontside of the play, the whole concept is designed to create a one-on-one matchup with the flanker. The skinny post by the slot receiver will search out the empty space in the between the safeties in the middle of the field.

At the same time, the underneath defender who would normally be in position to undercut or double the curl route is influenced by the skinny post route or the flat route coming underneath him.

Spot-Dig Concept w/ TE Motion

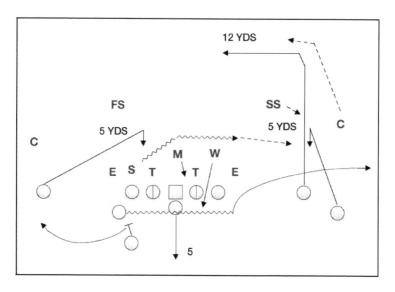

The offense toys a little bit with the vertical route on this concept. Where normally the vertical route ends up breaking deep and to the outside on the corner route, this time the receiver breaks across the middle on the dig route to take advantage of an open middle of the field, especially against the kind of pressure the defense is bringing on this play.

The tight end comes in motion from left to right, and brings the Sam linebacker with him, where he was originally creeped up into the A gap. The flat route by the tight end ends up being the hot route when the defense comes on the overload pressure like in this example.

The Z receiver setting the "pick" to provide a good seal on the play and allow the tight end to catch the ball and turn up the field for a big gain. This is especially the case since the corner would usually be playing deep to that side is chasing the dig route by the middle receiver.

For all intents and purposes this is a "bunch" play that is trying to create rubs in the passing game while creating enough spacing between the three of them. The late motion by the tight end to turn the right side of the formation into a three-receiver si forces the defense to react quickly, and adjust their coverage accordingly.

To the left side of the formation, we see the single receiver run a wider version of the drag-hook that the Z receiver on the right is running. This is similar to how a lot of offenses will tag the backside receiver with a slant route when running some kind of spacing concept.

The most valuable things about the way this play is designed are that it provides an answer to most coverages or pressures that the defense can throw at the offense, and because the vertical receiver running the dig route in this concept breaks a tendency, and therefore makes sitting on routes and pattern reading much more difficult.

Z Deep Cross X Dig

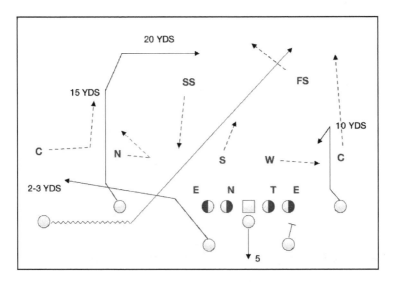

If you're a coach who loves to run a lot of crossing routes over the deep middle, then usually there's a second part to that equation, namely, how do you remove or other account for the defender to that side of the field?

Most of the time, it's a pretty straightforward answer, with the offense running some kind of vertical route to the opposite side to occupy the deep defender and take him out of the equation so that the deep crossing receiver gets to the space with no one in front of him.

Here we have the opposite approach. Instead of running off the corner to that side, the offense will try to get him to clamp down on a short curl route while bringing a deep receiver from the opposite side of the field to come over the top of him.

Also built into the concept is a dig route further to the left coming across the field at a 20 yard depth.

Finally, the flat route coming from the backfield gives Warner a good outlet against the blitz or in case the day routes don't come open for whatever reason.

6
RB PASS ROUTES

In the late 1990's and early 2000's, the premier back in football was a guy named Marshall Faulk. He could do it all, running, catching, you name it.

In Faulk, Mike Martz had his X-factor, the guy he could line up anywhere on the field and threaten defenses with, and he put him to good use.

Over the next few pages we'll dive into a few examples of how Faulk was used in the passing game, and how the Rams were able to maximize their already impressive and incredibly talented back.

Tailback Smash

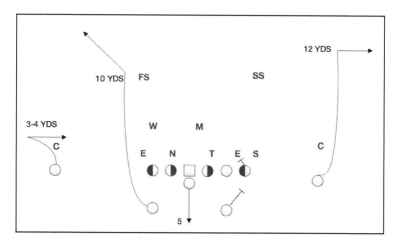

Here's a holdout from the old BYU offense back when LaVell Edwards was still calling the shots, and proceeded to influence much of the next generation of coaches.

Using a two-back formation like this puts defensive coordinators in a bind, since Faulk lined up in the backfield (in an offset position like you see in the diagram) is only a couple of steps away from a standard 2x2 one-back set, but at the same time, he's still in a position where he can take a handoff and get involved in the run game.

The world application of that idea is that a defense who likes to base their calls off of the pass strength of the formation has a quandary. Of the three guys lined up on or near the line of scrimmage, the pass strength is technically to the right side of the formation.

However, when you've got a special player like Marshall Faulk who is a threat to catch the football wherever he is, and has the speed to run vertical routes from the backfield as if he was lined up in the slot, you have the ability to create matchup problems that defensive coordinators don't have to deal with very often.

Here's the situation: Faulk is running a corner route out of the backfield, and he's almost certainly going to get favorable coverage with the right kind of leverage on the route. If he doesn't, it's likely because the corner playing over the top of the X receiver drops to take away the corner route by playing outside leverage deep, which of course means that the underneath route by the X receiver will be open.

Starting from the backfield does mean that the Will linebacker usually starts tighter in the box and with inside leverage, which opens up all kinds of space to the outside for Faulk.

The Will's alignment is dictated by the two-back formation, similar to the kinds of problems that a two-back formation with Faulk and all his pass-catching abilities and explosiveness can create.

If I'm Mike Martz and I start to see the Will backer cheating to the edge to get an early jump on the pass routes, I'm going to line up in the same formation soon after and call a run play up the middle where that linebacker should be standing. If the Will is vacating his gap on the inside, make him pay for it with something like a lead draw play to that side. Anytime you can force the defense to be wrong and punish them for playing unsound, you should do it.

Texas

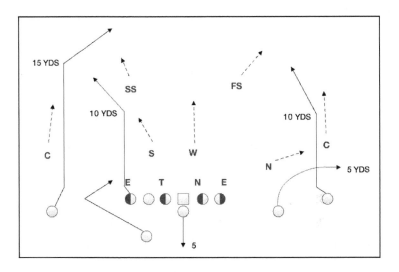

This particular route out of the backfield is a great adjustment to defenses who like to use their underneath defenders, especially linebackers, to crowd the deep middle of the field and try to take away the vertical passing game. One of the most common versions of this strategy is referred to as "Tampa 2" coverage, where the middle linebacker drops into the deep middle, the vacancy between the two safeties, so that the offense can't attack that area as easily just by throwing a post or a seam route right down the middle of the field.

Of course the disadvantage to this strategy is that the defense is now playing with fewer guys underneath, leaving them vulnerable to routes like the one drawn up in the diagram.

The angle route by Faulk is specifically designed to attack and replace the space in the middle of the field where the linebacker used to be, and the corner route from the tight end should be carried by the Sam linebacker, which means that Faulk should have free reign underneath once he catches the football.

This play was a staple of Bill Walsh's West Coast Offense back in the 1980's when Roger Craig was playing the same kind of position that Faulk was playing with St. Louis. Bill Walsh loved to throw the ball to the backs, particularly Craig, out of the backfield on a regular basis. The concept was called 'Texas' and it's been co-opted and duplicated over and over again by people at all levels of football (as all successful schemes are).

The play perfectly suits Faulk's abilities as a receiver at the running back position, and it's a scheme can be packaged with all kinds of peripheral route concepts to attack down the field and stretch the coverage.

The switch-up between the corner and post routes down the field is a perfect example of that. The combination is designed to attack down the field, and specifically put the near safety in a 2-on-1 situation. Adding routes like this to the play is a great way to give Warner some options in case the defense doesn't do what you anticipated, or they're just intent on not allowing Faulk to catch the ball out of the backfield.

To the opposite side, the post-flat concept has the potential to spring a receiver open, particularly the post route, since once he clears the flat defender there will be a window for the football to come his way.

Tailback Seam/ TE Angle

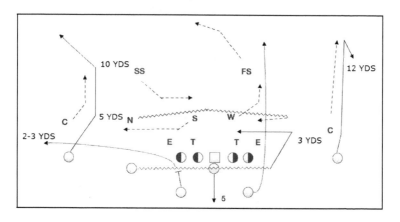

Here's another way that St. Louis uses the tailback in the passing game to attack the middle of the field.

The tight end start flexed out to the slot on the left, going in motion from left to right before coming to rest in a short split outside the right tackle.

What happens next is almost like an exchange of routes between the tailback and the tight end in the Texas pass concept.

It's important for Warner to survey the defense's reaction to the motion. In this case, the nickel corner chases the motion all the way across the formation, and the two inside linebackers stay in place. This should be a huge giveaway that the defense is playing man coverage, and Marshall Faulk will be matched up on the Will linebacker.

Either way, the defense leaves the middle of the field open underneath, but compensates by rotating the strong safety down into the deep middle in the robber position.

Tailback Divide

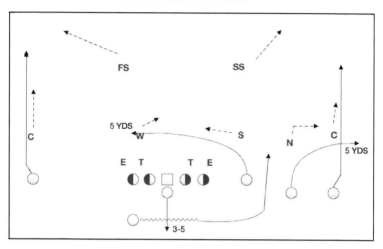

This play is the answer to the question, "How do we create a lot of space for our best player in the middle of the field?"

The flip by Faulk from the left side to the right side of the formation plays a big role in the success of the play, since now the offense can flood the same side of the field with four receivers, but the routes are separated and designed to isolate the route by Faulk on an unsuspecting defender, or even better, possibly defended by no one at all if the defense doesn't do a good job of adjusting.

First, let's talk about the shallow route by the

tight end, since this route can tell us a lot about the philosophy of the play and what Mike Martz is trying to do here.

The tight end's route is designed to create as much horizontal spacing between the defenders as possible. There's a reason why the tight end isn't going vertical on some kind of seam route or deep cross. It might be easy to look at this play and wonder why there are no vertical routes challenging the deep middle of the field. The reason is because the emphasis is on creating space horizontally and making the tight end available to catch the pass right away.

Think about it this way: If the tight end is running vertical up the seam, for at least the first 5-7 yards (at least) he's trying to evade and get past the first level of the defense, and he's not making himself a huge target for the quarterback either. What's more, he's still not creating an opportunity for Faulk to make a huge play after the catch, which is key.

What does one have to do with the other? Let's go further.

If the tight end runs a vertical route here, and the ball is thrown to Faulk, the defenders chasing the vertical route are still standing between him and the end zone, and will likely come off the vertical route, forcing him to move east and west, looking for the next crease in the defense, and meanwhile he's lost all the speed and momentum he built up coming out of the backfield in the process.

Now let's be clear. There are plenty of pass concepts that use this kind of philosophy where the QB will search the number of vertical routes available to him before checking the ball down to the back coming from his spot in the backfield underneath, and it can be a very effective way of keeping the defense in check and moving the football when you have to. That said, it's only a route that the quarterback throws when he's all out of options. The back is a checkdown, an afterthought, in those plays.

That's not the case here.

Faulk is not a checkdown, he's one of the primary receivers on this play. If Warner can get him the football in stride, it turns into a footrace to the end zone, and in this particular situation

Faulk has been coached up to head straight to the middle of the field since the two safeties are busy doubling the vertical routes out to either side, so there's a giant gap in the middle of the field with his name on it.

Just like the shallow crossing concept that we'll cover later on in more detail, there is a big "clearout" principle that is central to this play. When an offense is running a receiver on a shallow crossing route starting from one side, generally they've got a package of vertical routes to the other side of the formation to clear out the space for the crosser once he catches the football and begins to turn up field to get yards after the catch.

It's the same principle here.

The offense is trying to clear out the space as quickly as possible, and that means when Faulk is running north and south, the rest of the receivers should be running east and west so that they're all running on different planes, and it adds a lot of depth and width to the concept.

The more separation between the routes, the

better, and the success and explosive nature of this play depends on it.

7
CROSSING ROUTES

What do you do when you've got a collection of speedy receivers, a quarterback who can get the football out of his hands accurately, and a defense that is intent on not giving up the deep ball?

Start throwing crossing routes of course.

Crossing routes in the passing game are also a great way to clear up any doubts as to the coverage. It's a lot easier to figure out whether that corner is playing man or zone if he's chasing the receiver across the field during the play.

Ultimately, like everything else in this offense, it's

all about matchups, and finding ways to take advantage of them, and the crossing route concepts are no different.

If you've found a way to get your receiver matched up on an inferior corner, instead of trying a low-percentage pass deep down the sideline, why not run him across the middle on a crossing route that takes about the same amount of time to develop (sometimes even less) and get a much easier throw for your quarterback?

Does it make sense now why the Rams use this concept?

Drive Concept

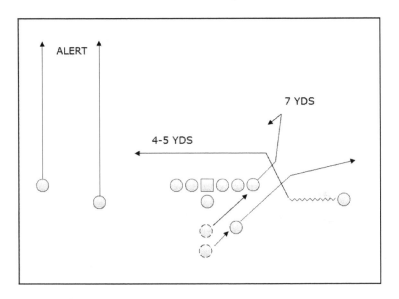

The offense starts off in an I-Formation before moving into a one-back set with Faulk offset to the strong side. This gets the offense into a cheap version of a bunch alignment, at least once the Z receiver comes in short motion into a tight split off the hip of the tight end.

To the opposite side of the play, you've got a pair of vertical routes. To the outside, more a fade technique, to the inside, a seam route with an inside release that creates some spacing between the routes, and puts a defender, like a linebacker, flying out into the flat for instance, who wants to try to play both route, into a tough situation.

The inside receiver should also be ready for a ball thrown his way once he clears the 1st level of defenders, especially if he sees the defense comes with pressure at the snap.

It's true that either of these routes can in theory hit deep, but the inside break of the route by the slot receiver brings him a little closer to the passer, so he's in a better position to grab anything thrown his way.

It's also obvious that the two vertical routes are designed to clear out any underneath coverage and open up the field for the shallow crosser once he catches the football so he can turn the corner and get upfield with having to slow down and make a more dramatic cut.

To the three receiver side, we see the offense create bunch look that is designed to release one of those receivers against man coverage. There's a method to the madness as well, since the receivers have a specific order to release it into their route. It's drilled and timed up, otherwise you'd be in danger of having these guys run into each other and screw everything up.

The tight end releases outward and gets on top of the shallow-crossing route so that he can create a rub on any defender in tight coverage.

This is why most corners will start to back off and create a cushion between themselves and the receiver once that receiver goes in short motion and gets into a tighter split, especially when it results in a bunch look. He doesn't want to put himself in a position to get picked by trying to cling tight to a receiver running an underneath route, and he also doesn't want to open up a large open space in the area behind him where the offense can throw a corner route or some other vertical pass once he's pressed up at the line.

Finally, Faulk breaks out to the flat as the ultimate checkdown, a guy who can turn two yards into twenty with just one broken tackle. In many offenses, that flat route guy is the third option in the concept, but because of the kind of player they have in Marshall Faulk at that position, it's not unusual for this offense to call this play in short yardage situations and get him the football as soon as he breaks wide to the flat.

For young quarterbacks, it's important to drill a specific progression of receivers into his head, just as a starting point in their football education. However, for a guy like Warner, who is smart enough and talented enough to get the football out in time to just about anywhere on the field, and he's aware enough to realize the situation and when/if the defensive rotation dictates that the football should go somewhere else.

Bunch Shallow/ Deep Sit

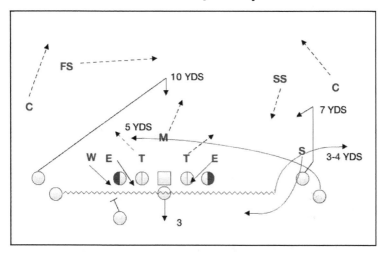

This time around, the offense has the same idea, but moves the "bunch" out wider, separating the "spacing" concept from the rest of the formation.

The slot receiver comes in motion from left to right, and plays the part of the flat route, as opposed to the offset back.

In this particular situation, the defense comes with a zone pressure that drops both of the defensive tackles into the underneath zones that can interfere with the shallow crosser or slant routes that could be coming from the receiver on a tight split.

The deep sit route by the X receiver serves to help clear out the coverage to that side, as well as present a secondary option behind the crossing route.

This is a classic passing concept that's been used by many successful coaches, including Bill Walsh, and is a good complement to the shallow cross route that's used by a lot of teams these days.

The offense starts off with stacked receivers to both sides before bringing the slot receiver to the right to force an adjustment by the defense, either by chasing him with a defensive back in man coverage, or in this case the safeties invert and bring the strong safety down to the bunch side.

The Sam linebacker, who originally lines up over the point of the bunch to give a look like he's going to give some resistance in press coverage, but at the snap he comes wide off the edge.

The defense is hoping to force a quick throw to a hot receiver from Warner, who doesn't have a lot of options early on since the underneath route are so wide from the rest of the formation. Even the shallow crossing route that comes up open early is running his path right into the dropping defensive linemen. Ideally, the flat route is a good option, but it's such a long throw that the ball is in the air forever and it's at risk of getting intercepted by the strong safety.

Wide Receiver Flare Route

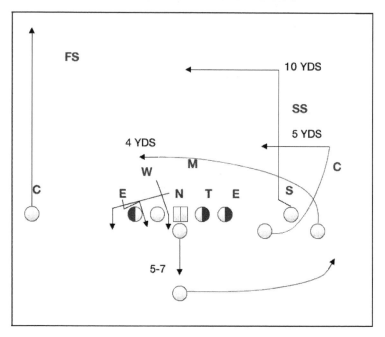

Here's an example of Mike Martz's genius in maximizing the effectiveness of the personnel at his disposal. On this play, he lines up the great receiver Ike Bruce alone in the backfield in the tailback spot. For one thing, it gives the defense something brand new to look at, but the other positive aspect is that when combined with the bunch alignment gives the Rams a creative way to get the football to one of their most productive playmakers right away and hopefully give him the opportunity to create something out in space.

The pass concept also takes four receivers and floods a specific area of the field with them. Just to stay even in the numbers game, the defense would have to commit four guys to that side, but most defensive coaches prefer to outnumber the offense in the pass game to both sides. The Will linebacker coming on the blitz does put some pressure on Warner, but also leaves the defense a man short in coverage.

To the single receiver side, the fade route by Torry Holt occupies the corner and the free safety, and opens up that side of the field for the shallow crosser, who in turn is both working as a viable receiver but also running interference on the middle of the defense.

To the bunch side of the formation, the Rams are running the 'levels' concept, with the inside man running a more rounded shallow crossing route than in the traditional concept.

Warner can read this play from left to right, since each route breaking in at each interval is designed to take advantage of open space and also create space for the next route coming in behind him.

Even if Bruce is lined up in the backfield, Warner could find it more advantageous to get the football to someone else, like the dig route breaking over the middle depending on how the strong safety reacts on this play.

Putting your playmaker in the backfield, especially as it relates to the passing game, can be incredibly effective, just like we discussed on an earlier play, and Martz is an expert at moving the playmakers around, considering how much talent he has available to him.

Mesh/ Wheel

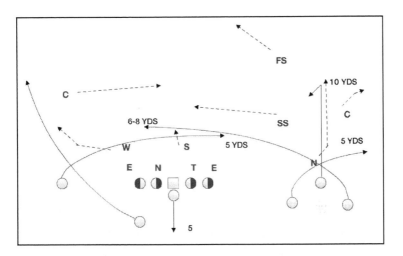

This time around the offense puts two different crossing routes on the field with the single purpose of creating a rub on the defender chasing the X receiver in man coverage. The play is set up to allow room for the shallow route by the X receiver to come open against zone coverage as well, since the wide alley created by the split by the bunch and the right tackle.

By forcing the flat defender to widen out and press the point of the bunch, the offense can create a lot of space between the numbers and the middle of the field. Once the X shallow cross route clears the Sam linebacker's location he should throttle down a little bit and look for the football.

The curl route by the receiver lined up at the point of the bunch can also come open late depending on the leverage of the nickel corner in coverage.

The wheel route by Faulk comes open past the original alignment of the X receiver. One of the mistakes players make on this route out of the backfield is slowing down and looking for the football once they get past the line of scrimmage right away. As a result, they end up slowing down too early by turning around and looking for the football early. Receivers who look for the football too early and slow down are a big reason why quarterbacks overthrow their intended targets and the football ends up in the hands of defenders.

Shallow Flood Concept

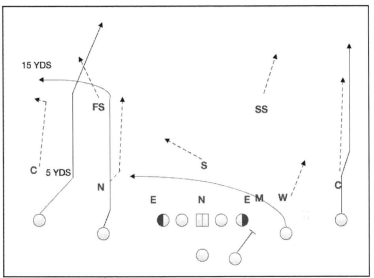

The route combination to the left side of the formation is specifically designed to build on the clear out concept to the opposite side of the shallow crossing route.

After running the same shallow concept over and over again multiple times (which this offense had a habit of doing), you need to find ways to change it up and give the guys in the secondary different looks.

The passing concept is designed to squeeze the coverage to the deep left, and as the X receiver breaks to the inside, the corner starts to peek at the vertical route by the #2 receiver, waiting for the two routes to switch.

It's important to emphasize that the shuffle technique by the corner in zone coverage makes it easy to sit down on any out-breaking routes, as well as keep an eye on the drop of quarterback to key in on when to expect the football.

Defensive coaches have something called the "movement area," where between 10-15 yards past the line of scrimmage the defensive back should expect the receivers to make their break, to whichever direction they intended to go. The reason it's such a reliable key is because the depth of the routes time up with most 5-7 step drops when a quarterback drops back from center (the rule holds pretty consistent when the QB takes the snap from the gun as well).

All the while, the slot receiver to the right side is coming across the middle, and he gets the catch at the other end of the formation.

This where the corner's technique comes into play.

Because the corner is shuffling while gaining depth, he's keeping an eye on the play developing underneath, he flies downhill once he sees the football headed to the shallow route, and once the catch is made, he's in position to force the receiver to change his path, lose his momentum, and have to change his direction, which funnels him back closer to the rest of the defense.

8
SCREENS

A well-designed screen package is built around already existing concepts in the offense, so that not only is it a great tool against an aggressive pass rush, it's an effective way to complement the things you already do well.

In this chapter we'll go over some ways that Mike Martz used specific formations and motions to force the defense to show their hand, and get numbers to the point of attack.

You'll also see how by adding run action and pulling linemen, the Rams were able to build a screen play that looks like a run concept from the shotgun, almost like some of the more modern college-style spread option attacks that you can see today.

So let's get started.

Trips Tailback Screen Weak

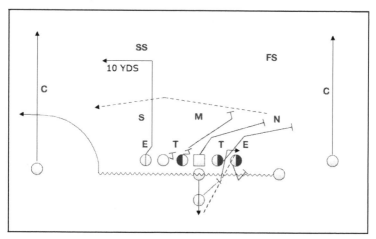

This is a play that revolves around the offense's ability to create extra space in the alley to the weak side. By lining up in a 2x2 set, then motioning the slot receiver to the left, they're watching for the reaction of the nickel corner, and the defense in general.

The defense is likely going to adjust to a motion across the formation, either by moving the nickel corner lined up across from, or by rotating the near safety down into a position down low over the three receiver side.

Ideally, Martz would like the nickel to chase the motion to open up space underneath, but even if he stays still, the offense has the numbers to that side of the play when both guards and the center fly out to the alley to seal off the nickel and turn away any defensive linemen chasing the play from behind.

To the three receiver side of the formation, you've got a standard flood concept by the Z receiver going vertical, the Y receiver cutting out at 10 yards to take advantage of the vacated space cleared out by the Z receiver, and the flat route by the slot receiver controls the underneath coverage and/or provides a checkdown/hot route in case of a blitz or something unexpected.

The vertical release by the Y receiver takes away the Sam linebacker as he carries the route deep, and the Mike linebacker is matched up in man coverage, so he's chasing the screen play the whole way, but the convoy to the right side clears a path for Faulk in the alley.

I Formation Flex Screen Weak

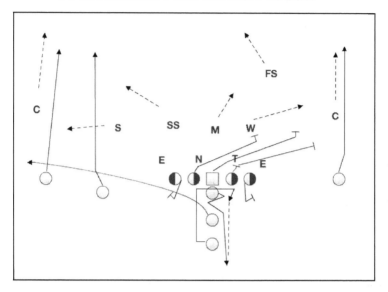

This is a similar theme to the first play we talked about in this section, since the formation creates space to the right side between the right tackle and the X receiver in the alley.

Martz has designed another great way to get the football to Faulk out in space, this time with the help of a play action fake from Warner in the backfield. By taking part in the play fake in the backfield to the left side, the slipping to the right at the aiming point behind the right guard.

The backfield action with two backs lined up in

the I-formation gives the defense a great picture and even more than that, the vertical routes from all three receivers give Warner a place to put his eyes. The quarterback's eyes are an underrated part of the screen, as well as other types of misdirection plays, since by eyeing a particular route or defensive player, he gives a more realistic picture for a vertical pass that makes such a big part of this offense.

The fullback runs out to the left as part of the backfield action when Kurt Warner fakes it to the left, almost like a power play, and he leaks out to the left flat as an outlet that hopefully takes away some of the underneath defenders.

The technique from the offensive tackles to either side isn't quite the same screen technique where they open up and invite the pass rushers outside of them, but they do went to engage with them and guide them to where they want them to go.

Trips Shallow Cross Screen Weak

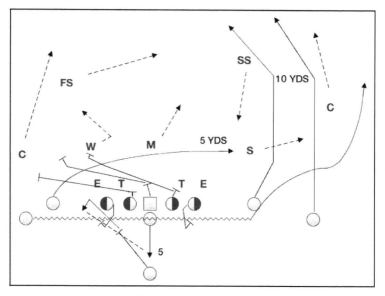

This play continues the trend of attacking the single receiver side of a formation, and also uses motion to identify the coverage and create extra space to that same side.

The offense moves to a 3x1 set with the motion man finally coming to a stop on the inside hip of the tight end who's flexed out.

The drag route from the single receiver side gives the defense a crosser to be worried about, as well as possibly creating a rub on the middle linebacker, as well, as possibly influencing the CB on the FS depending on the coverage.

It's common for defenses to leave their corner on an island to the single receiver side of the trips formation in order to use the free safety to cheat over the top of the third receiver on any vertical route coming from that side hat intersects with the free safety's location.

The screen to the single receiver side is actually paired with a vertical passing concept, as the double post routes are designed to hi-lo the near safety. The drag route coming from the backside also comes into play late, as it gives Warner something to look at while he's timing up his drop and the throw to the tailback.

If everything goes according to plan, and the defense plays as expected, the corner drops to his deep zone, the Will linebacker drops wide to cover the opposite flat, and the offense has a 3 on 2 advantage to the screen side.

Faulk should be wary of the rush coming from the backside defensive end, since it could interfere with his aiming point where he's supposed to set up in the backfield and look for the pass. He should assume that the path of the defensive end will take the left tackle far up the field, so he should be ready to set up to the left, feigning as assignment on pass protection, and then once the tackle has invited the pass rusher up the field, he'll find his spot right where the pass rusher used to be.

Warner should be dropping back and be ready to drop the football to Faulk after the fifth step, and bring careful to not put a lot of air on the pass. Faulk gets the football and has another opportunity to make a play out in space.

Counter Throwback Screen

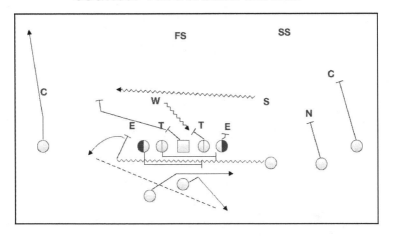

This is a great reason to use pulling linemen to set up a pass away from the backfield action.

Warner carries and the wide play fake to Faulk who runs on a track like he's getting out to the edge on the stretch play. Meanwhile Warner comes out of the fake and stays on track to head to the edge, and almost as if he's waiting for a receiver to come open down the field, and at the last moment he should turn and get the football back to the slot receiver on the left side just as he's coming open.

The slot receiver comes in motion from right to left, making a stop off the hip of the left tackle, presumably as the cutoff man on the backside of a counter play. Until other screen plays in the section, this play is paired with a run look. As a result, there is no downfield pass threat to occupy the secondary, because even the fade to the backside receiver is only because of the press coverage by the corner, otherwise the receiver would've just sought out the corner dropping back and giving the receiver a nice cushion.

The motion by the slot receiver brings another defender (the Sam) to the side of the screen, but the center continues on his path up to the 2nd level after blocking back on the nose, and the right guard would've done the same if in this particular situation the Will linebacker isn't creeping up into the right A-gap.

For argument's sake, you could easily line up Marshall Faulk in the slot to go in motion and catch the pass, but most of the time this is a play used to get the football to guys like Torry Holt or Az-Zahir Hakim who may have trouble getting the football because the defense is doing a particularly good job of taking them away that day.

This is another hallmark of the Martz offense, where he has many reliable ways to get the football to his playmakers, and has answers for an aggressive defense.

9
GADGET PLAYS

While not exactly their bread and butter plays, the Rams did occasionally throw a trick play or two at their opponents.

Mike Martz was one of the most creative football minds in the league in his day, and a great example was the way he chose to keep opponents off balance are plays like the ones we'll go over here in this final chapter.

Shovel Pass

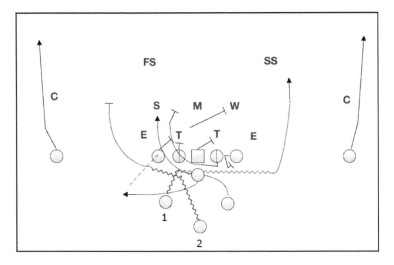

There are two different men going in motion at two different times here, so it's obviously very important to get this play called and get the players out of the huddle as quickly as possible. These are marked in the diagram in order by the numbers 1 and 2.

The offense lines up in the full house diamond formation, and once everyone is set, Warner sends the left up back in motion to the right, where he'll stay flexed out as a receiver.

Once he's set, then Warner sends the tailback in motion out of the backfield and to the left, where he comes to a stop just off the outside shoulder of the left tackle.

At the snap, Warner sprints to the left with the right up back coming underneath him and following just behind the pulling guard. As for the tailback starting out to the left, he will widen out and serve as a lead blocker out on the edge. Depending on how the unblocked defensive end reacts, Warner will either shovel it to the up back, or keep it himself and get what he can around the edge.

Since Martz isn't drawing up these plays with the intention of creating running opportunities for Warner, the Rams are obviously hoping that the end comes up the field, which will open up space for the shovel pass behind him.

A coaching point on the right up back on a path out of the backfield is to stay behind the pulling guard on his path as he's pulling around the combo. The right up back, who could end up catching the shovel pass depending on the reaction of the defensive end, should stay patient behind the guard, at least until the quarterback makes his final decision on whether or not he's going to keep the football or shovel it.

If he does receive the shovel, he should stay tight inside of the B gap, since it's likely that the Sam linebacker has overrun the play, following the flow of the backfield. His emphasis should be on aiming "inside-out" while keeping an eye on the near inside linebacker.

If the defensive end closes down the line, squeezing down and taking away the shovel pass, the quarterback should already be wide enough so that he has the space to get vertical immediately.

Obviously since Kurt Warner is the quarterback taking snaps, he's not the ideal ball carrier. Martz would rather see the football in Faulk's hands, and that's usually how the defense ends up playing it.

This is a way to help slow down the vicious pass rush that defenses bring in Warner's direction. The upfield path of the defensive ends have to be slowed down in order to make this offense as effective as possible.

If St. Louis can negate the effects of the front

four when it comes to rushing the passer, naturally the defense will have to commit extra bodies to rushing the passer, which in turn leaves more room in the secondary for the receivers, and St. Louis will win in that situation more often than not.

Empty QB Draw

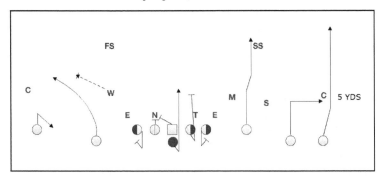

This particular play wasn't a huge part of the Rams' offense, but it's a logical adjustment to the many defensive coordinators who aren't concerned at all about Warner's legs.

These days it's rare to see a defense lines up this way, especially with the quarterback lined up under center, but on the list of things that defensive coaches are worried about, Kurt Warner running wild on the defense is not high up on the list.

The draw play is packaged with a pair of passing concepts, one on each side. It's another example of playing the numbers game to either side.

If there's a middle linebacker, or some other defender sitting in the tackle box taking away the middle of the field, it's up to Warner to find when the defense is short by a man, and get the football to that side.

This is another advantage of keeping the quarterback under center. Warner has the ability to get yardage right away. If he was lined up in the gun, that's 4-5 yards he has to make up before he gets positive yardage, and meanwhile that gives the defense enough time to react and fly to the football.

It also takes away the effectiveness of any defensive line stunts, since by getting downhill and into the A gap, the defensive tackles don't have enough time to twist and exchange gaps, and if they attempt it, it may end up being an even easier block up front, since the offensive line may end up coming the football while the defensive line is standing up and putting all their weight on their back foot leaving them vulnerable to someone with more force and better leverage.

It's worth mentioning that Warner doesn't get vertical right away, similar to the way you run the quarterback sneak, but drops back two steps to give the defense a pass read, and then get downhill into the A gap.

The interior offensive line's responsibility is very simple. The nose tackle gets doubled by the center and guard, since defenses put their big run-stopper at nose in the A-gap. To the other side, the right guard should block on the 3 technique tackle long enough to take him out of the play, no matter where he goes. If he slants inside to the A gap, the guard should wash him down and Warner should widen out his path. This is another reason why it's an advantage for warner to drop back for a couple of steps before getting vertical, since it lets the blocking develop.

Warner may not be the definition of a mobile QB, but he's still athletic enough to make a defense pay if they're not paying enough attention to him.

The "Oh S***!" Screen

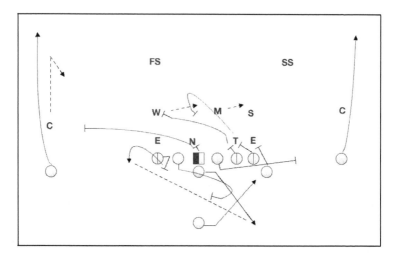

This play is nicknamed the "oh s***" screen, because of the defense's collective reaction once they see the football going the opposite direction.

It's a perfect example of using a tackle-eligible play to throw an unsuspecting pass away from the flow of the defense. Though it's possible to line up a tight end at that spot and throw him the football, it's far more effective when you've got an offensive lineman there so the defense isn't expecting anything thrown that way.

In order to make him eligible to catch a pass, the tackle first has to check in with the officials as he comes on to the field and let him know that he will be taking the place of an eligible receiver on the field. The referee then gets on the PA and announces the substitution to the crowd and to the defense. In other words, the defense knows he's there, but still they're expecting a run here.

Still, after he lines up, the X receiver has to come off the line of scrimmage, and the Z receiver lines up on the line to the opposite side of the formation. This makes him eligible to catch a pass, while still keeping enough men on the line of scrimmage.

In order to bring attention to the right side of the formation and away from the offensive tackle eligible to catch a pass, they line up the pair of tight ends in a wing alignment to the right side.

This gives the defense a very good visual cue that the strength and the area of emphasis should be to that side.

To bring even more attention to the right side of the formation and away from the eligible tackle side. Warner opens up to the right and runs to the mesh point out wide to meet up with the tailback (Faulk) before setting up and looking downfield as if the offense is taking a shot down the field.

At the last minute, he turns and peels back to the left side as the offensive lineman comes out of his block, reversing out and presenting his numbers and giving Warner an easy target.

The guards play a large part in the play. To the frontside, the right guard pulls wide as if the offense is running the stretch play to the perimeter, and the left guard starts to pull wide in the same direction as the stretch play, then as he crosses the center, he begins to rotate clockwise and pull to the right to set up as a blocker for Warner as he sets up at his new spot deep in the backfield.

As the play starts, the tackle starts to hinge block, protecting the inside gap, perhaps inducing the defensive end lined up over him to try to beat him inside, thereby opening up space for the screen outside of him in the left alley.

The center blocks back on the nose before climbing to the second level to set up a wall for the screen, and the two offensive tackles blocking down on a combo of the defensive tackle lined up over the right tackle, and they also use their path to climb and add to the wall of blockers on the left side.

This works best in the red zone, on the goal line, and in short-yardage situations.

ABOUT THE AUTHOR

Alex Kirby is a former high school and college football
assistant who now writes about the game he loves at
ProFootballStrategy.com and LifeAfterFootballBlog.com. He
lives and works in Indianapolis, Indiana.